The Seasons

by

Gregory Opstad

Finishing Line Press
Georgetown, Kentucky

The Seasons

Copyright © 2025 by Gregory Opstad
ISBN 979-8-88838-936-2 First Edition
All rights reserved under International and Pan-American Copyright Conventions. No part of this book may be reproduced in any manner whatsoever without written permission from the publisher, except in the case of brief quotations embodied in critical articles and reviews.

ACKNOWLEDGMENTS

Sucker Lake Portage, 1956; Poem Beginning with a Line From Robert Bly; and Safe Harbor originally appeared in *Lake Country*.
A Walk in the Woods originally appeared in *Tiny Seed Literary Journal*.
Wintering won 2022 Honorable Mention in Lake Superior Writers Annual Short Fiction Contest

Publisher: Leah Huete de Maines
Editor: Christen Kincaid
Cover Art: Stanley Opstad
Author Photo: Jennifer Hoffman
Cover Design: Elizabeth Maines McCleavy

Order online: www.finishinglinepress.com
           also available on amazon.com

                Author inquiries and mail orders:
                       Finishing Line Press
                           PO Box 1626
                 Georgetown, Kentucky 40324
                              USA

Contents

Wintering 1

Late Winter, Early Spring 8

Paddling my Canoe 9

Night Fishing 10

Into Summer 11

A Walk in the Woods 19

Rubus Parviflorus: The Common Thimbleberry 21

The Bear 22

Spring Arrival 23

Sucker Lake Portage, 1956 30

Poem Beginning with a Line from Robert Bly 31

Portages 32

Autumn Changes 33

Sucker Lake Portage Redux 42

Lake Superior in Autumn 43

Safe Harbor 44

Wintering

The needle on the thermometer outside on the window frame rested on the peg at minus fifty degrees. It wouldn't get any colder than that, he thought. He wouldn't go outside today. There was plenty of wood in the box.

He scuffed into the kitchen to make a pot of coffee. The bottoms of his Steger mukluks made a shushing sound as he moved. With the woodstove stoked, the cabin would quickly warm up. As the coffee perked, he looked around with a feeling of satisfaction.

His father and older brothers had built this place. They started from scratch by clearing the woods for a driveway. They staked out the perimeter for the cabin, felling trees with their one chain saw, building the cabin by hand. The cabin overlooked a glacial lake, three miles from the Canadian border. It took almost nine hours to get there from their home in Minneapolis. It was quiet up there, no cars or lights, hardly any other people. He only saw trees and water. He was seven then, in 1955. A city boy, he was awed by the wilderness. He spent whole summers at the cabin, learning about the woods. The cabin passed from the family sometime in the 60s but he never forgot about it.

Now 75, he was looking for solitude so he could write. There was plenty of quiet here. He bought the cabin back a few years ago, taking time to settle in. It met his needs now. There was still no electricity, with only a Franklin stove for heat. Water came from a well, pumped into the cabin. He used kerosene Aladdin lanterns for light. It was just what he wanted.

He sipped his coffee, staring out at the white expanse. The storm had blown for hours during the night, high winds shaking at the very foundation of the cabin. The windows rattled. The outside door banged. There was a constant roar, like a train. It was a serious storm. He couldn't see anything outside during the storm. Snow pelted the windows. It held his attention all night. He hadn't slept much, listening to the wind.

There were no tracks visible the next morning. Even the woodpile was covered, likely three feet of fresh snow. The snow's surface was littered with pine needles. Branches broken off by the wind were scattered across the ground. The sky was clear and sunny. As it always did, following a blizzard, the temperature dropped. He had prepared for cold weather like this. He had put up an ample supply of firewood for the winter. Estimates said he'd need six to eight cords, split and stacked, but he put in ten.

The first flurries came in mid-October. A few flakes from an overcast sky, melting as they hit the still-warm ground. There would be more bright days ahead. The snow wouldn't last. By Halloween, however, after days of cold with no sun, it started snowing in earnest. He decided it was time to move his car to the lodge for the winter. This is it, he thought, this snow will last. He'd made arrangements with the owners of the lodge to park his car in their lot, told them he'd be back occasionally to keep the battery charged and to drive into town. After parking the car, he walked the gravel road back to the cabin. It was snowing hard by the time he got back. He stoked the fire, mixed a drink, and sat down to read by candlelight. By morning there was a good eight inches on the ground. Winter was here to stay.

On warm days, with temperatures above zero, he'd ski along the trail he made through the woods and on the lake. He needed the sunlight and fresh air. There were only a few hours in the day when this was possible. It didn't become light until around nine. The sun went down by four. The short days reminded him when he'd walk the few blocks to school, dark both ways in the dead of winter.

He spent weekends in the fall splitting firewood. The sound of the maul on the wedge rang through the woods. It brought a pair of Canada Jays to the nearby trees. They squawked and chittered, hopping from one branch to another, each time coming a little closer. He occasionally tossed bits of food out for them, which they greedily grabbed. They flew it to their cache somewhere in the trees. They'd be back for it later, when forage was scarce. These birds planned for winter, saving food in caches all around their range. The Native people called the jays wisakedjak. The lumberjacks heard this as whiskeyjack. The name stuck. These birds have always been camp followers. They got along well with people. He was happy to leave them tidbits of food. The chickadees were also attracted by his wood splitting. They'd be on hand to sort through the splintered bark for larva and insects even before he went inside.

A big storm is coming, he thought. He'd seen a ring around the full moon the previous night. Today there were high cirrus clouds. He could feel the barometric pressure dropping. The wind was building. He spent the day preparing. He filled the wood box in the cabin, checked his snowblower, had it ready by the front door. He wished he'd gone into town for groceries as he'd planned, but it was too late for that. There was still a little fear. A major blizzard was nothing to fool with.

In the old days his father and brothers would snowshoe up the lake carrying supplies in backpacks. They came up every year in March to shovel snow off the roof. He'd grown up listening to their stories of struggle in the snow, how they would stop by the first point of land along the lake to have a candy bar for energy, plodding through on snowshoes. They said one time that they couldn't make it all the way to the cabin. They weren't prepared for how hard it was to break trail. They had to break into another cabin down the shore for shelter. He never knew if they'd really done that. His brother told him how they once tried to build a fire along the way but snow from an overhanging branch fell, snuffing out the first warming flames. He was pretty sure that story had come from Jack London. In any case, coming up in the winter sounded like a romantic adventure to a little boy.

He wasn't entirely alone. No neighbors in winter, but deer were plentiful in this taiga. The bears, occasional in the fall, had long since gone into hibernation. Winter birds, of course, the jays, grossbeaks, the woodpeckers, pine siskins, always the chickadees. Once he saw a great gray owl sweeping silently over the snow in an open area, hunting. Plenty of birds to keep me company, he thought. And wolves. He'd never seen one but would sometimes hear them from a distance at night. In winter nature comes into its own, without much human intrusion. He felt the fine balance of wildlife and forest. Aldo Leopold would be satisfied.

Whenever he went on excursions he took his backpack filled with extra clothes, matches, a battery, flashlight, and chocolate. He carried a little stove and a small pot with bouillon cubes, just in case. Tools included a buck knife and small saw. He hadn't had an accident outdoors yet, but with no one to count on but himself he had to be extra careful.

About once a week he went down to the lodge to start his car. Every couple of weeks he'd drive down the Gunflint Trail to Grand Marais for groceries and supplies. On those days he'd listen to MPR for the news. In town he went to the IGA for groceries, the municipal for wine, lunch at the Gunflint Tavern. A beer and a little companionship. The town had grown from a little fishing village in the 50s to a lively artist's colony now.

When not bringing in wood or skiing on the lake he stayed bundled up inside. With no radio or tv, no internet or cell phone, he had a good supply of books, a stack of notebooks and pens. A typewriter, but no computer. Old school. He had plenty to do. He worked on his poems every day, made notes in his journal, kept track of the weather. Often, he would write by candlelight, a fact that pleased him.

The original cabin had been on land cleared by hand. His brothers even had to build a road into the place. He'd heard stories about how they dug the footings by hand, some six feet down to get below the frost line. Since it was originally intended to be just a summer home insulation was minimal. The cabin, sitting in the middle of the woods was well-shaded. It seemed that it was always cold, even in the summer. Before his father put in their own well, drinking water came from a neighbor's. At first there was a large icebox outside but a bear tore that apart one night. It pulled the icebox over, peeled off the doors, working to get to the food kept inside. The outhouse, a one-hole structure on a path 20 yards into the woods, was a scary trip at night.

He had no reason to go outside now. He could wait until it warmed up before digging out from the storm. It would still take him a few days. Given the extreme cold it was too dangerous to clear a path now. He thought of Jack London again.

His childhood backyard had been lakes and forest. He had the freedom to make his own trails through the woods. He had a favorite rock where he could sit and be mad at his sister. By the time he was twelve he was allowed to take the canoe down the lake to hike portages to the neighboring lakes. There was an occasional bear. Deer were fairly common. A northern boreal forest, the whole area now was part of the Boundary Waters Canoe Area Wilderness. Permits were required to even hike a portage. His lake was an entry point into the BWCAW with two extensions at the end where outboard motors weren't permitted. Things were different now.

The cabin was different, too. Modernized. The interior had been properly finished. There was a real bathroom. They had put in a composting toilet, so trips to the outhouse in the middle of the night were a thing of the past. The cabin finally had a real kitchen. Despite the lack of electricity, it was a fully functional modern house. Bookcases lined the walls. Here, in this winter, it was comfortable.

There'd been plenty of snow before this blizzard, deep enough for his ski trails to become passages for deer to favor. One time, on his way back to the cabin, a large doe blocked his way. He'd never seen a defiant deer before. He stood in front of the animal. He waved his arms. The doe refused to move. She stared back at him, glaring. He could see hot breath coming out of her nostrils. He shushed and shooed it but the deer just pinned her ears back. She stiffened her legs. Only January and she'd had it with this winter business, the cold, the deep snow. She refused to step off the trail. He finally lifted his shoulder, raised his arm, and wedged his way past the deer. He didn't want to touch her for fear of causing her to bolt or kick. Being even this close was risky. He lifted his ski pole over her head and along her back. He leaned over more than the deer did. He made it past the animal, kept on skiing, back to the cabin with a warm fire waiting.

    The wind had died down. The sun was out. A bright calm seemed to spread over the new snow. He finished his coffee and fixed some hot oatmeal and toast for breakfast. Maybe he'd do some writing today. It was very cold outside. At least fifty below.

Late Winter, Early Spring

The day is cold, the sky gray,
rain drizzles through empty branches,
the hesitant beginnings of new buds
giving shape to the wind. Tree
limbs litter the ground, lay across
decaying leaves, a delicate interlace
of mycelia spreads as snow mold
rings unmown blades of grass.
Hoary crystals melt as the rain
dissolves a lingering bank of snow.
For the first time in months the
air is alive with smells, dank,
but not unpleasant, earthy. Morning
frost disappears, life begins to stir.

Paddling my Canoe

I move across the surface,
silently, slowly, paddling
a j-stroke here, balancing
on the wind to keep
a steady course.
I have to correct,
pull harder on my j,
adjust my course.

Here I cross the lake,
headed into the wind,
my bow too high,
pushing me to the side.

Again, I correct, pulling
forward, alone on the water,
getting there by aiming upwind,
allowing the boat to angle down,
down towards the portage,
down to my landing.
I lay my paddle athwart
the gunnels, resting.

Night Fishing

After fishing into the night, I waited

for the morning to clean the fish.

Two good-sized walleyes

left on the stringer, gone in the dark, victims

of a clever mink, fed by my indolence.

Into Summer

It was hot, hotter than usual. Pine needles steamed and gave off a pungent smell. The balsams bubbled with sap and gave off the scent of Christmas trees. The leaves on the aspens were turned inside out with the expectation of rain. The path to the lake burned the children's feet as they ran down to the dock. They would remember this day.

They danced with anticipation as they waited for their parents, one of them anyway, to come down to the lake and watch them as they splashed in the icy lake. A good day for swimming, more than just a dip in the cold water. The dense forest shrouded the cabin. It kept the daytime temperature cool enough but swimming was still a treat. The glacial lakes, always thought to be pure and clean, had millions of years of leaf and bark residue suspended in the water, still, always refreshing

Cousins, three of them, a boy and two girls, made little boats out of boards and bark, floating them around the dock. "The S.S. United States!" declared one. "America! Mine's the America!" shouted the next. Only a few miles from Canada, they were conscious of borders and boundaries. Bored after a few minutes, with nothing to do except skip stones across the water, the children bickered and argued, waiting for the adults. They wanted to swim.

When the adults showed up, the children donned their life vests, slipped into their sneakers for the sharp rocks, and jumped off the dock. The cold water was a sudden shock but they didn't mind. There was a drop-off close to the shore that they were cautioned about but they ignored that.

Taking risks, they splashed further and further out, past the safety of the shore. The kapok life vests, remnants of WWII, were not safe. Adult sized and worn out, they quickly soaked up water and provided only the illusion of protection. They always left the wearer vulnerable.

The boy went too far out, past the drop-off, and began to sink. He panicked. Looking through the murky water he saw the white legs of his cousin swimming by. He reached out and grabbed her foot. Startled, she pulled up and kicked, propelling him towards the shore. He found the bottom and kicked up off the rocks. He managed to scramble back to the dock. He was scared. Swimming wasn't fun anymore. He sat on the dock, shivering from the close call, not the cold. So easy to just slip under the water unnoticed until later when it was too late. So easy to be missed in the excitement and fun. Drownings are usually quiet affairs, hardly ever the splashing and waving you see on television. This time he was lucky. The life vest, useless in any case, hung on his thin shoulders. It dried, slowly, in the sun. He didn't go back in the water that day and never mentioned the incident to anyone.

After days of hot weather, it was time to go into town and get more ice for the coolers. Their fathers fished every day and fresh meat came from the lake in the form of walleyed pike. The daily catch was plentiful but they needed to resupply the larder with other perishables from town. Trips into town were always great fun, a change from the isolation of the wilderness cabin. The Gunflint Trail was a narrow and winding gravel road, wide enough, usually, for two cars to pass but travel was slow. It took over an hour to drive the thirty-some miles into the small fishing village.

The children, wearing only shorts and tank tops climbed into the car. They looked forward to the adventure, seeing other people, getting groceries, and, hopefully, a treat from the Ben Franklin store. They stared out the car windows hoping to catch a glimpse of a black bear or deer along the side of the road. A nickel for a deer, fifty cents for a bear. They were usually disappointed but always had their hopes up.

Down the street, at the end of Wisconsin Avenue, past the Ben Franklin to the end, they could stand on small rocks on the shore of Lake Superior, smoothed and rounded over the millennia. The stones made a soft clacking sound when you walked on them. The water lapped at the stones, small waves washing over them. These were perfect for skipping, but not today. There was a big dip in temperature after the last drop from the hills above Lake Superior. Grand Marais was cloaked in fog. Barely fifty degrees, it was a disappointing cold that greeted the half-naked children. Barefoot and shivering, they huddled together, wanting now to just get back in the car and go back to the lake, thoughts of treasures from the dime store forgotten. After getting groceries and picking up the ice, the trip was over. Driving back to the cabin, they could smell the change in the thermocline. The cold air warmed, became hot again as the car went back up the hill. They could smell the pines, the needles, the pitch bubbling and steaming on the trees. The day was perfect again.

He remembered that smell as he sat on the dock. No need for fishing today and, despite the uncommon heat, no need for a dip in the lake. He was past that now. The cabin in the woods sat on a hill above the lake. It was a short walk down the path. The day was ripe for sitting, listening to the water lap against the rocks. He was in no hurry. Thoughts of his once-proud little boats plying the shallow water reminded him of how he and his cousins once played. Too many years had passed. He looked across the lake at the opposite shore. The reflection of leaves from birch and pine blurred as soft waves blended the images. They looked like coins stacked up, moving and shifting with the movement of the water, he thought. Coins along the bank, he thought. Coins in the bank. He smiled at the little joke.

A pair of loons swam by, diving and resurfacing before him. Excellent swimmers and even better fishers, they dove below the surface, appearing as if by magic somewhere else on the lake. Their young, two of them, were about twelve weeks old, fully fledged. They paddled further out from the adults. By summer's end they would find their own lakes for nesting, find their own partners. But for now, on this lake, still connected to their parents, they were content to stay relatively close. There was a mournful cry. And another, further away, from a different pair beyond the little island down the lake.

His thoughts moved back and forth through time. Each movement, every tree, the sight of the reflections of the leaves along the shore held memories for him. He could see where he had his close call, just past the drop-off when he floundered under the water and his cousin, unknowing, saved him. Across the lake was a portage to the next lake just to the north of them. There was a stream, a waterfall that connected the two lakes.

Another big adventure was to climb the waterfall. It was a small stream, a passage from one lake to the next. The challenge was to make it to the top without falling into the water. They docked at the portage landing, then hiked through the brush to the mouth of the stream. There were large boulders, mossy wet rocks, and deep pools coming downhill from the lake above them. Logs and deadfalls sometimes blocked their way. The children scrambled and jumped from one rock to another, climbing slowly up to the top. Invariably, one child or another slipped and fell into one of the pools. The others would laugh. No one was ever hurt and it was all in great fun. There was a marshy area at the top of the waterfall. Soft muck to sink their feet into, willow branches to sweep aside. Once at the top, the children would make their way to the boat landing at the end of the portage. The hike back down, taking the portage route, was somewhat easier but tree roots stuck up on the path were still occasion for caution. Rocks, smoothed over by generations of canoeists, worked their way to the surface. It was dark. Trees were tall and shaded the trail. There was little in the way of underbrush and they could see far into the dappled forest. There was always the worry that they'd encounter a bear on the path. They never saw one but the delicious fear stayed with them until they reached the boat landing on their lake and they could jump into the boat to be forever safe.

One time the boy's older brother went along with them. While the children climbed the waterfall he carried his fishing rod for casting on the other lake. He spent an hour casting for northern pike. The sky darkened and a fierce thunderstorm broke over their heads. Lightning flashed all around them and the children were frightened. They were soaked by the rain so it didn't matter if any of them fell into the water along the way. They shouted for the brother when they got to the top but he had already gone back down the portage. He waited for them at the landing. Cold and shivering from the rain, they wanted to get back in the boat and go home. "Are you crazy?" the brother shouted over the rain. "With all this lightening you want to get in a metal boat and go out on the water? That's crazy!" They waited until the storm passed.

Whole summers were spent at the lake. The children learned the paths through the woods, animal trails mostly, deer tracks. They could wander where they wanted, no adults around and be home by supper time. They could take the boat out on the water as long as they wore life jackets, the ones from Army surplus and WWII. No matter. They were careful. They only went out on the water when weather was good and boating was safe. They fished on their outings but never caught anything. One time they found a boat that had floated loose from someone's dock. They left it alone but told their parents who then went around to the various cabins along the shore until they found the owner. The adults were relieved that it was only a loose boat and not one where someone had fallen in and was lost.

They built forts out of deadfalls with brush for roofs. Secrets were told in these forts, some kept still to this day. They would huddle into the narrow, dark spaces and tell stories of their great adventures.

He sat on the dock in the afternoon sun. It was pleasant to sit and do nothing. He may have dozed a little bit and he might have done some meditation but, for the most part, he just looked at the lake, listened to the breeze, and smelled the pine trees all around him.

On sudden impulse he stood up and walked over to the boat rack by his dock. He slid his aluminum canoe into the water. Life jackets, good ones this time, and paddles, were always handy. He picked up his fishing rod to take along. Sitting in the stern, he pulled a strong j-stroke with his paddle and moved quickly out onto the water. He steered along the shore until he had an upwind angle for the portage. His strokes were strong and even. His paddle made no noise and he moved without splashing, a skill honed from many years of canoeing.

The canoe moved slowly past a small island. From where he sat in his boat he could see the open spot on the hill to the southwest side of the island. There was still a patch of wild daisies growing in an open field. He smiled as he remembered the family claiming that patch as their own some seventy years before, naming the place. Other people, over the years, had likely given the island their own names but in his mind it was still and always would be Daisy Island. He paddled the canoe now across the open water between the island and the portage. The wind had come up a little and there was a slight riffle across the water. Not whitecaps yet, but they showed the possibility. He felt good, being on the water, being in charge of his little boat. It was good to paddle across a lake.

He edged the boat to the shore as he passed the outlet from the waterfall and approached the landing. Without any fuss he landed the boat against the dock. He threw a line around a piling and lifted himself out of the canoe. There was a sploosh as his weight shifted to the dock. He tied the line off and took his rod with him as he walked the portage. There was a lure still attached to his line. No need to climb the waterfall today, he thought. He set off into the darkness of the portage. His steps were steady as he walked up the hill. He scanned the forest as he walked, still on the lookout for bears. He noted the remains of ancient canoe-rests nailed onto trees and saw the new ones put up by the Forest Service. The portage was 120 rods long and canoeists were happy to have these crosspieces to lean their canoes against as they rested along the portage.

He sat down on a boulder as he reached the landing. He set his rod on the ground and contemplated the opposite shore. The color of this lake was a little more green and the other side had more dead trees lining the edge. It had always been this way, he thought. He watched the ripples on the water and listened to the wind through the trees. There was no need for him to cast his lure. He was content to just sit and appreciate the lake as it was. He had strong feelings for these lakes. He'd spent his childhood in these woods and on these waters. It was where he went in his mind when he needed to relax and reflect. There was no other place for him after some seventy years of a busy life. He prized his memories. He enjoyed the solace and peacefulness this place brought. Now, in his later years, he was grateful to actually be there in person. He was at home today. It was a fine afternoon.

After some time, he picked up his rod and headed back down the portage. It was getting late and he wanted to get back to his cabin. The sun was turning the sky a golden color as he pulled the canoe back up on the boat rack. He took his fishing rod with him as he went back up the path to the cabin. It was time to fix a little supper and then maybe do some reading.

A Walk in the Woods

First, you notice the smells, moist pine needles,

bits of bark and twigs, a kind of bitter smell that fills

your nostrils and swells your heart. The air is heavy

and lush. A piney forest, damp with the morning air,

fresh and ancient at the same time.

Note the colors,

mostly green

with dots of white,

trillium

and wood anemone,

thimbleberry buds.

Green

and white, then,

but mostly green.

                        And the sounds, the occasional

drumming of a grouse, the warbles and dee-dee-dees

of the smaller birds. Once,

along this path, there was

a blur of black, a bear

sleeping just off to the side.

You gave it a wide berth,

went another direction.

But it's the smells in a damp forest

that keep your attention,

not exactly rot or mold

but still . . .

Rubus Parviflorus: The Common Thimbleberry

thumb sized

brilliant red

nestled in green

from tiny seeds little druplets

tart

fuzzed

picked from bushes that drape the woods

a celebration   a few

for a treat a little for now

white flowers

repeating and again

The Bear

sat waiting in the bushes,

sated from its raid

the night before

and liking what it found.

I propped open the screen door

knowing it wouldn't stop him anyway.

The sheriff's deputy identified him

as the one prowling

elsewhere, preferring

a fresh pan of brownies

over Cindy's tomato basil bread.

Spring Arrival

He thought about waiting until ice-out but, by then, everything would be muddy and awful. Maybe he should leave while things are still mostly frozen. Ice-out wouldn't be until May, half the spring gone. The lake would turn gray with the ice gradually melting out from the shoreline. There'd be no more skiing around the lake. He could still ski through the woods, though. Even with daytime temperatures in the 50s, the shade-covered snow would last into June. The deer were gaunt, haggard. After the blizzard in January, deep snow piling up, feed for the deer was scarce. Branches higher up on the arbor vitae were gnawed. His wood pile was pretty thin, too.

He started closing up the cabin in April. It was a gloomy season. Rain, most days, cut the snowdrifts down, melting them into muddy puddles. During the winter he could ski right from his front door but now he had to walk his skis out from the cabin to the trailhead down the way. Too much walking around in the clearing by the door had ruined the trail. He went out on his skis every couple of days, but warm weather was starting to favor red klister which had all the elements of trying to spread honey on his skis. Once out, however, he could ski in shirtsleeves. He had his favorite route, about five kilometers, staked out between the trees, up towards a neighboring lake and back. It was a good run, quick, that gave him just the right amount of exercise. With the changing of the seasons and the longer days, he had more time to clean up the yard. He retired the snowmobile. He changed the oil and cleaned the treads. He covered it with a tarp. He'd use the ATV for trips down to the lodge now. He hated to use either machine. The harsh motor sounds grated in the wilderness. Not so with his skis. He loved the quiet while skiing. The trails he'd made along the shore and through the woods were still good, but with better weather, he could go out for hikes along the road, too.

He wrote some poems over the winter. He organized them in alphabetical order. Then he reorganized them according to topic and theme. Finally, he made a sort between the ones he would keep and the ones he would put on the bonfire. Of the dozens, he kept only ten. He had a few short stories. He would keep those. They were good. In years past, he'd go to the post office in Grand Marais to mail out his pieces but now most everyone wants on-line submissions with Submittable. He didn't have an internet connection here at the cabin. Hell, he didn't even have electricity. When he got back to the Cities he'd email everything off to various journals and hope for the best. Some of them might find a place out in the world.

Today was bright and clear, a change from the gloom of spring rains. He went for a walk down the road. There was little chance of a fall but he still wore his backpack with emergency supplies. He wasn't skiing and the road was smooth. There were about a dozen summer homes along this road. They were all built around the mid-1950s, rustic cabins without plumbing or electricity. The land was leased from the DNR, the hundred-year leases still good for a while. Some of the driveways had cute little signs with names for the cabins, like "Thimbleberry" or "The Shack" but his family never did that. One of the places had a chain across the entry with a sign saying "Private Keep Off." They made jokes about that place, assuming the owner was retired military personnel and proud of his rank. The road itself was minimum maintenance. Side growth extended out over the driving lane, only about one and a half lanes nowadays. He saw a deer one time on this road, a large male with a huge rack of antlers. It walked slowly towards him until it was just a few yards off and then it stepped off into the woods, no hurry. There were plenty of hoof marks in the mud today. The snow in the woods was still deep. It was hard for the deer to navigate the forest.

In the early days they would fill water bottles from a neighbor's well. The lake water was presumed clean but they only used that for washing. His father eventually put in a well, sharing the expense with the neighboring cabin. That made things a lot easier. As a child he was tasked to carry the water from the well. He filled one-gallon buckets and carried them back to the house one at a time. He was little. It was a struggle to carry those pails. The pail was measured in U.S. and Imperial gallons. He wondered why they were marked that way. His father must have bought those pails in Canada. He must have spilled at least half the water lugging it back to the cabin. Now, with the new system put in by a previous owner, the cabin was fully plumbed and there was no need for carrying sloshing pails of water.

His other job was to fill the kerosene lanterns. There was a shed on the other side of the driveway where gasoline and kerosene were stored. He'd set each lantern on the turn-around rock in the driveway and carefully pour the kerosene. You don't always notice how quiet things are when you're busy. You're just focused on the task. One time, however, he noticed that it was very quiet while he was filling the lanterns. No chirping or chittering of squirrels, no songbirds making noise. He finished his job and walked the lanterns back to the cabin. As he got to the door, he turned and looked behind him. A black bear was following his trail. He hurried inside.

His parents sold the cabin in the early '60s. He missed the place and always wanted to return. He found the current owners a few years ago and made a good offer to buy it back. Various owners had modernized it over the years but had not ruined the rustic charm he remembered.

The previous owners had left behind some books. He added to the collection since he bought the place, making quite a library. He'd read some of the books on the shelves but he likely wouldn't ever read everything. It was just a comfort for him to be surrounded by so many books. The cabin was cozy, walls lined with books and pictures, windows overlooking the lake. He had his poetry. Novels he'd read years ago and would read again. Hemingway, Steinbeck. Joseph Heller. Kingsolver. Classics. There weren't any mounted deer heads or bear rugs. No stuffed animals at this cabin.

He bought a pot roast on his last trip to town for groceries. He'd gotten lazy the last few weeks and resorted to meals that were filling but not satisfying. A real meal with meat and potatoes with gravy would be ideal. Cooked carrots. A fresh salad. That's what he'd need to counter all the dreary weather. Most of his meals were simple. He cooked on the propane stove. Spaghetti. Soups. Hamburgers. Once in a while a meat loaf. What he'd have at home, if he were there. But a pot roast was something to look forward to.

The weather reports didn't predict any change. It might rain the next few days, cloudy in any case. He kept a log of daily temperatures and days without sun. The coldest he saw was minus fifty degrees, that one time after the blizzard. It could have been colder but that was as far down as his thermometer measured. The temperature didn't rise above zero for ten days after that. Regular high temperatures were around seventeen degrees below zero and the lows were in the minus twenties. The longest stretch of overcast weather was fourteen days. It snowed a total of fifty-two days over the winter. Completely sunny days were rare. He was used to darkness. With spring coming, the days were becoming longer and brighter. The sunshine improved his mood.

He wanted to explore along the road. His hike was easier now. He decided that he didn't need his backpack. He stuck to the high side of the road to avoid the mud. It felt strange, to be away from the cabin without the backpack. On every other excursion, snowshoeing or skiing, he carried tools, a saw, extra batteries for the flashlight, matches, clothes. Chocolate. Always chocolate. The pack was heavy but he thought it was necessary to have these things just in case. Today, though, with little chance of breaking a leg, he didn't think he needed it.

The road was muddy, as he expected. There were patches of snow that would likely remain until June but his hike was mostly clear. He saw deer tracks in the mud but didn't see any deer that day. He counted the other summer homes up to the end of the road and then headed out through the woods. This was a trail he sometimes skied during the winter. The trees weren't budded out yet. The balsams gave off the scent of Christmas. He came across a portage he'd forgotten about. It was a short one, a rough path, really, leading to the next lake. It wasn't a popular lake, just another in the seemingly endless strings of them. He turned left and followed the trail. He'd never taken this portage. The trees were thin and the forest was open. The ground, still frozen, would be marshy and wet when it thawed. The shoreline around the lake was starting to melt, the edges black and the ice rotten. The lake was small and mostly round. He wished he'd come this way earlier in the winter. It would have made a nice run on his skis.

He walked around the lake. There was a large deadfall and a blowdown of smaller trees that looked like it could conceal a bear's den. He saw tracks around the opening, a sign that a bear had wandered out once in a while during its slumber. There were other signs of wildlife here. A winter forest is never still. It abounds with life, every day. Tracks crisscrossing in the snow, chewed twigs and branches. A springtime forest is the same but you can't see the signs as clearly. Today, aside from the bear and deer tracks, there were the faint scratches of voles and squirrels across the muddy surface.

There was a beaver lodge just off the shore. The water around it was open. Beavers were active, moving in and out of their den. It was good to see all these signs of wildlife. Relatively close to human habitation and yet living undisturbed by man. He was glad to know it was there. He would stay away from that lake in the future, not wanting to disturb them.

He found his own footprints in the mud as he returned to his starting point. He backtracked until he was on the road again. He'd had some exercise and found a new place in the woods. That was always a good thing. The sky began to cloud up. It started to rain. The temperature dropped. He quickened his steps, anxious to get back to the cabin. The rain turned to snow, a hard spring squall. The puddles on the road were crusting over. There was going to be a shift in the weather, a shift for the worse.

He was soaked by the time he got back to the cabin. He was cold and shivering. He raked the coals in the fireplace and put on some new wood. Soon, the fire was blazing and the cabin was warm. With a change of clothes, he sat in front of the fire, clean and dry. He took a short nap. The sudden storm, in the background, raged for a while and then quit. He was ready to start the pot roast.

Sucker Lake Portage, 1956

Seeing the darkness

framed by sunlight

surrounded

by thistle and thimbleberry,

it became a tunnel through which

I had to pass.

From the open field I follow

its path

twisting

down

through.

Into

trees and leaves and shadows shimmering:

an underwater world.

Diving into emerald radiance,

I hold my breath

and swim.

Poem Beginning with a Line from Robert Bly

And my old fishing line driven up on the rocks . . .
was what I thought about as we drove in hasty
silence back home. I'd snagged it on a branch,
it snapped; I was unable to retrieve it; the black line
spun off my reel and left to tangle with decaying
branches and fallen leaves washing the shoreline.
My fishing pole was tossed in a corner of the one-room cabin,
forgotten, as my parents threw clothing in the car.
A ranger had just brought news of my grandfather
and there was a seven-hour drive. Soon my line,
the branches, those leaves, would be frozen
in the November ice, but for a few more days
they would still splash against the rocks.
For now, there is just the yellow wash of headlights
aimed away from the lake as the family
began to gather in the cold night.

Portages

Gateways to other lakes, trails through the woods marked by rustic signs, measured in rods. Three of them on my lake, each one to lakes far different than the one before and portages from them to others. The closer one, climbing up from the very first step, steep, high, tracing along a waterfall, one lake to the next like ascending a flight of stairs, a green lake named for a crocodile, long and narrow. The easy portage, short, flat, walking on soft pine needles leading to a rustic scene, a small lake, round and easily crossed. A moose stood in the shallows. From there, through a narrows into a panorama, a huge lake with high, rocky palisades, islands and bays. You could spend a month and never repeat yourself, Little Alder into Big Alder, Flour to Moon. Another, through the woods into a clearing with old buildings, walls falling down and bleached white from the sun, a logging camp that was abandoned before your parents were born, then into the forest again, greens turning dark, down winding stairs, twisting and turning, a labyrinth of trees to another lake. I went from lake to lake as a child, my backyard playground that now requires permits to even land at the dock.

Autumn Changes

He had been talking about the place for years. It was where he spent his summers as a child back in the 1950s. He never forgot about it. He told stories about it. He dreamed about it. Now it was time to go back and find it again.

He invited a friend to drive to Grand Marais and go up the Gunflint Trail. It would be a trip to renew old memories. It would be an adventure. He'd been back in this area many times before over the years. One time he stayed at the lake's campground with a group of friends. They walked down the road and found the cabin. No one was there so they walked down the path to the lake and watched the sun go down from the dock. Years later he showed the place to his wife. Again, no one was there. They walked around the cabin, taking it all in, remembering. He hadn't been back since, almost twenty years.

He and Gerald left early one morning in late autumn. Coffees in the cupholders, granola bars for energy, he picked his friend up at his home outside of Duluth. They chatted as he drove. It was a casual conversation, the comfortable talk of old friends. They were both familiar with the route to Grand Marais. They'd each traveled up the shore many times over the years. It was a lovely day. Just a bit past prime leaf watching, the colors were still good. The autumn storms hadn't yet gathered over the lake, tearing the leaves from the trees. The sun shone across Lake Superior. Hawks were gathering along the shore, not wanting to venture out across the water on their southward migration.

He thought about his parents and their trips up there in their younger years. Highway 61 wasn't even paved past Two Harbors. It was a rugged gravel road back then. They did primitive camping on lakes along the Ely/Finland Tail. His parents and an aunt and uncle, the four of them, had a tent and a few blankets. They carried sacks of flour, some coffee, and a few cans of beans. They fished for dinner. Old-time fishing outfitters would leave rental boats at various portages but his parents would lug their rowboat over the portages to get across the next lakes. They'd often camp two or three lakes in from the road.

As children the family was all packed into the car. The children were excited for the trip up the north shore. From Highway 100 in Minneapolis to Highway 61 through Cambridge to Askov everyone played the alphabet game. Letters were called from roadway and fixed signs along the way. The first person who called a letter from a word on a sign could claim it and the first person to get through the whole alphabet won the game. His older brothers started cheating, picking letters from the names of passing cars, f in Ford, g in Dodge. The boy was annoyed with his brothers, as usual. Once they crossed the Kettle River on Highway 23, their father declared that they were in the Official North Woods. A dime to be for every deer they saw, a quarter for each bear. He pressed his forehead against the window, peering. He never collected on the challenge.

The ore docks were located in the west end of Duluth. Rail lines merged there with gondola cars filled with taconite ore for shipping on Lake Superior downlake to the steel mills in Ohio. Rail cars moved slowly along the high bridges overhead. One by one they gradually advanced their loads until dumped into the holds on the ore boats. It seemed to take forever to drive through the West End. Traffic was slow and the children just couldn't wait to get to the cabin. Finally, at the east end of the city there was a quick sighting of Lief Ericson's statue before leaving town and finally up to the north shore. The family took pride in their Norwegian ancestry in the Viking ship that had been built in Minnesota and once sailed to Norway. It was later returned to Duluth and put on display in a park along Lake Superior's shoreline.

They counted the sights along the shore that marked the way. Castle Danger, Split Rock, Temperance River. Sometimes they'd stop at Russ Kendall's Smokehouse in Knife River for smoked fish and beer. They sat on the rocks by the lake. The boy, too young for beer, dipped a cup into the lake for fresh water to drink.

Silver Bay was another slow spot, new housing developments bursting in town for the employees at Reserve Mining. He saw the taconite refineries and the odd green color in the water where the Company dumped the tailings from their mines.

The Gunflint Trail was one of the more well-known Boundary Waters locations. It was a sixty-some mile route through the woods leading to lakes on either side. It went all the way to the Canadian border at Saganaga Lake, a haven for campers, canoeists, and fishermen for almost a hundred years. In the early years it literally was a trail used by loggers. Fishing camps were developed over the years with rough cabins built for fishing outfitters. In his childhood, the road was a barely two-lane gravel road, not paved past Grand Marais, winding through the woods. As an adult, with the road straightened and paved, wide enough for Winnebagoes and fifth-wheel campers, he and his family went up the Trail for camping and fishing.

There used to be signs along the Trail, mileage markers for each of the lodges along various lakes. As a child, he watched for each one, counting down the lakes before getting to the one for their cabin. Those signs were long gone but he knew very well where to turn. Or at least he thought he did. The lakes were the same but some names were different and he missed the first turn. When it became obvious they were on the wrong road they turned back. They found the road down to the lodge. It was narrower than he remembered and brush along the sides grew out into the road. The sign for the summer homes wasn't there any longer. The road itself looked abandoned. Suddenly he wasn't certain where he was. He worried he might not even be able to find the cabin. He'd been away too long. They turned down the road to the campground.

The water was dark and a little foreboding but it was the right lake. He saw a sign with a map showing portages, islands, and landmarks. The road he was looking for wasn't named but he found it on the map. They drove back to that turn and began working their way towards the summer home area. There wasn't anybody around. The road was in poor condition. Nothing looked right. He was worried again but as they crested a hill and turned to the right he saw the driveway.

Changes, yes, from over the years. The driveway was wider, more trees gone. The turn-around-rock that he used to climb up on was barely up to his waist. The cabin itself had been remodeled, twice the original size. The front door was in a different place. There was a storage shed where the outhouse used to be. The steps leading to the kitchen were different. But it was still the cabin he remembered, the place he still loved.

No one was there. Late fall, the place was closed for the season. The windows were boarded up, the boats up on the boat rack were covered with tarps. They went down to the lake. Everything was where it should have been. Daisy Island, up to the north, and beyond that the portage and waterfall where they used to hike. Across the lake, autumn leaves reflected in the gentle waves, looking like golden coins blurring back and forth. He took pictures and sat on the dock for a while, thinking.

A boreal forest, the landscape was a mix of pines and hardwoods. There were plenty of spruce and balsams. Spaced close together, these trees made for a thick, lush forest. In the fall, birch, aspens and poplars turned the forest a rich yellow. A soft shushing from autumn breezes through the trees made pleasant background music. This was a peaceful place.

Their drive back to Grand Marais was uneventful. As he reached the main highway he turned left to go into town but the signs were all off again. He drove a bit further and saw signs for the Canadian border. That was wrong. He was on the wrong side of town. He finally realized that the road up the Gunflint had been rerouted. He was disoriented again. He turned around and found the main street. They had lunch at the Gunflint Tavern where they usually stopped while in town. Lunch was good, the beer fresh. He asked for a friend, the brew master, but he had just left.

On sudden impulse, he drove around town until he found a realty office. He went inside and inquired about the possibility of buying the cabin, bringing it back into the family. The property had recently changed hands and the realtor knew which place he was asking about. His daughter was a realtor in Duluth. He left his name and gave the realtor his daughter's number, asking him to call her if a purchase could be arranged. He hadn't been inside the cabin for sixty years but that didn't matter. He wanted to buy the place.

His family was horrified at the thought of buying a cabin sight unseen. His daughter questioned the wisdom of such an act. His wife was against the whole idea. "We're in our seventies," she argued. "Why in the world would we buy a cabin in the woods?" He didn't care. It was the home he'd been searching for without knowing it.

He heard nothing about the cabin for months. It was always in the back of his mind. He bugged his daughter weekly, asking her if she'd heard from the other realtor but she hadn't. She was getting tired of his constant nagging. Finally, in the spring, she got a call. The current owners had hardly used the cabin at all since buying it and they were glad to have someone else take an interest in it. They began the negotiations.

He didn't think he'd need to go back and look at it before finalizing a deal but his daughter insisted. They went up as a family, his wife, his daughter, and himself. He was excited and couldn't stop talking, telling story after story about the place. His daughter was still skeptical but did her job as a realtor, making her assessment of the value of the property and what could be negotiated. She looked at the structure, its condition and what needed to be improved. She said that much of the value of a lake property depended on quality of the lake. He didn't need to be convinced.

He knew the lake and what its potential was. His wife noted that there was no electricity, no telephone, and no internet. Inside plumbing with a composting toilet and a pumphouse and generator for water, yes, but no modern facilities. He said he didn't care but he knew it would be a hard sell.

The cabin itself had been expanded from the original structure. It had two small bedrooms with doors that closed. That was different than the curtains hanging over a partition wall. There was a Franklin stove for heat. The main room had bookshelves with a few books, some mounted deer heads, and a lot of knickknacks. There was a couch, coffee table, and a couple of recliners facing the lake. It was small but cozy. The kitchen and dining room were in the addition. The stove and refrigerator were fueled by propane gas. The old picnic table was gone and in its place was a round dining room set. There was a hutch and regular kitchen cabinets.

Outbuildings included a storage building and the old gasoline shed, the place where he once filled the kerosine lanterns. It was still used for that purpose. The dock was new and quite sturdy. The one he remembered was made from the side of an old cabin his parents once floated down the lake from the site of an abandoned logging camp. They had to walk through this camp on a portage to another lake. He remembered as a child seeing the remains of other buildings. It was the place where his sister had once lost her sunglasses. He liked this dock better. Two rowboats and a canoe came with the property. The boats were on a rack that would allow the boats to slide into the water. There was a winch to pull the boats up and away from the lake.

His daughter thought the place was worth making an offer on but his wife was still unconvinced. He continued to point out the virtues of the place, the history of the area, that it was close to their friends' resort, up on Gunflint Lake. Even though he didn't really enjoy fishing, he told her about what a great lake this was for walleyed pike. He pointed out that the lake was a portal to the Boundary Waters Canoe Area, on the threshold of the last true wilderness in Minnesota. It was a hard sell but eventually he wore her down. She agreed to let him buy the place.

Once they made an offer, things happened quickly. They closed on the property in late June. So many papers to sign for such a simple transaction. He and his wife started moving in shortly after, cleaning out the taxidermy and knickknacks, changing out the furniture. They made it into a cozy den, books and couches and all. He started making plans for weekend stays, thinking this was just the place for him to get away from the world and do some writing. He wasn't bothered by the lack of electricity. He bought a manual typewriter and stocked up on notebooks and pens. His wife was secretly looking forward to his being gone, he thought. It gave her the time she needed for herself, too.

After weekends up there at first, he began to spend longer weeks at the cabin, writing, hiking, canoeing. He even did some fishing. He ordered firewood. He spent time cutting it into fireplace lengths. His stack of cordwood grew. It was hard work but it gave him plenty of exercise, a job he could do without having to think, the mechanical process of swinging the maul and listening to the ring off the wedge. The weeks went by and he was back into October again, a full year since he and his friend first made their trip up the Gunflint. He was no longer restless. In the back of his mind, he was already making plans for a longer stay, perhaps even a whole season.

Sucker Lake Portage Redux

Grasshoppers snapped
over the hot meadow
and black flies buzzed
around my head.
The open field
smelled like hay
wanting to be raked.
Sixty-five years
have passed
through this clearing
but I still cast my eyes
along the ground,
looking
for the sunglasses
my sister lost,
the pair she couldn't do without,
the pink ones
with the green lenses
and the sparkles
along the bows. I know
where they are,
right here
behind that bush,
or maybe somewhere past that tree,
there, just along the way.

Lake Superior in Autumn
Inspired by images of boats on water, untitled, by Jay Steinke

An equinox calm, a still-life in water and silver.

Boats sit as if suspended in milk. The lake is quiet.

No ripples, no movement. The sky, the lake, the air,

all white, all the same. Through the white scrim,

they appear, disappear. You can't be certain

how many there are. Sailboats on a languid tack,

a luffing sail, frozen in the foreground. Ore carriers

anchored further out are shrouded in . . .

. . . limpid images float out of focus. Five? Six?

Specks on a blank canvas, dotted images

in a milky setting, ships anchored in a cloud.

Safe Harbor

On the last hill down the Gunflint coming into Grand Marais, past the runaway-truck ramp but before the road to the landfill, you get your first clear view of the lake. The lighthouse is off to the left at the end of the jetty, the breakwater defines the edge of the little harbor. A few sailboats sit at anchor and gulls in flight become whitecaps out at sea. Down the shore, towards Lutsen, there's a thin, dark finger curving out and up, pointing to Isle Royal. It has a comforting shape, a tiny bay, a cove. I'd feel safe with my boat anchored there but water and sky are both so blue the little inlet is just a wisp of vapor, nothing really there, a trick of the eye, a mist, a safe harbor in waiting, never showing up until you actually need one.

A retired teacher, **Gregory Opstad** divides his time between homes in Cloquet, Minnesota and Cochiti Lake, New Mexico. He is a member of Lake Superior Writers. His poems have appeared in *The North Coast Review; The Rag; Migrations: Poetry & Prose for Life's Transitions; Trail Guide to the Northland Experience; Liberty's Vigil: The Occupy Anthology, 99 Poets for the 99%; More Voices of New Mexico; Manzano Mountain Review; The Thunderbird Review; Bringing Joy; The New Mexico Poetry Anthology; The Apaja'simk Journal; The Ekphrastic Review;* and *That's a Pretty Thing to Call It: Prose and poetry by artists teaching in carceral institutions*. His first chapbook, *Lake Country*, was released by Finishing Line Press in 2013. This is his second collection. His short story, *Wintering*, won Honorable Mention in the Lake Superior Writers 2022 Short Fiction Contest. *Bringing Joy* won 2022 Best Written Community Creative Work in the State of Minnesota, Minnesota Author Project Award.

www.ingramcontent.com/pod-product-compliance
Lightning Source LLC
Chambersburg PA
CBHW030100170426
43197CB00010B/1601